THE BATTLE OF THE ATLANTIC

The Longest Campaign of World War II

Written by Martin Wilfart
In collaboration with Antoine Baudry
Translated by Carly Probert

History 50MINUTES.com

THE BATTLE OF THE ATLANTIC

KEY INFORMATION

- **When:** September 3 1939 – May 8 1945
- **Where:** On the Atlantic Ocean
- **Context:** World War II (1939-1945)
- **Belligerents:** Allied navies (UK, Canada and United States) against the forces of the Axis, composed of the *Kriegsmarine* (Third Reich) and the *Regia Marina* (Kingdom of Italy)
- **Commanders and leaders:**
  - Erich Raeder, German Admiral (1876-1960)
  - Karl Dönitz, German Admiral (1891-1980)
  - Ernest Joseph King, American Admiral (1878-1956)
  - Sir Max Kennedy Horton, British Admiral (1883-1951)
- **Outcome:** Allied victory
- **Victims:**
  - Allied camp: approximately 45 000 dead
  - Axis camp: approximately 25 000 dead

INTRODUCTION

The Battle of the Atlantic was the longest World War II campaign. It mobilized extraordinary numbers, both of men and materials, in both camps and marked significant technical advances in many areas that would revolutionize naval warfare.

On 3 September 1939, at 9pm, just ten hours after the proclamation of the state of war between Britain and the Third

Reich, the *Athenia*, a British ship weighing 13 500 tons that travelled to New York, was torpedoed by the German submarine, the U-30. Of the 400 people onboard the *Athenia*, 122 died. These were the first victims of a campaign that would last 68 months, and which would see thousands of ships sink, killing tens of thousands of sailors.

The outcome of the battle was extremely significant. The Germans wanted to gain supremacy in the Atlantic Ocean in order to prevent the British from receiving aid from the American continent and the British colonies. They hoped to strangle the British, the only opponents of the Nazi regime in Europe after the surrender of France in June 1940, and force them to surrender in turn. However, although it was effective, the German strategy, mainly based on the use of submarines, would not bend the Allies, who managed to transport men and equipment in order to undertake the conquest of occupied Europe.

POLITICAL AND SOCIAL CONTEXT

THE PREMISES OF THE SECOND WORLD WAR

The Battle of the Atlantic, its outcome and its development can only be understood by placing it in its much wider context: the Second World War. Although the war officially began on 1 September 1939, when Germany invaded Poland, this conflict had its roots in the more distant past. Several factors thus caused the conflagration of the world, including:

- The implementation of decisions taken at the end of the First World War, which were endorsed by the signature of the Treaty of Versailles in 1919. The terms of the agreement imposed very heavy economic, military and territorial sanctions for the conquered states and were the source of a rise of resentment and a desire for revenge among the people who had lost the war.
- These feelings allowed for the emergence of nationalist political parties and even parties with totalitarian tendencies, which aimed to find the glory that would have been lost during the armistice of 1918. Thus, Italy saw Benito Mussolini (1883-1945) take power with his Fascist party, gathering the people who were disappointed by the outcome of the First World War because they believed that, although Italy was on the winning side in 1918, the peace negotiations did not provide any advantage.
- The economic crisis that began in the U.S. in 1929 quickly spread and ruined the economies of industrialized countries within a few months. The effects were particularly

devastating in countries that were subject to the harsh conditions of the Treaty of Versailles. Therefore, this crisis, combined with the vengeful feelings of the population in 1933, allowed the Nazi Party led by Adolf Hitler (1889-1945) to gain power in Germany.

- The expansionist wills of men such as Adolf Hitler and Benito Mussolini, which pushed them to want to acquire new territories. In Nazi Germany, this was the Pan-German movement, which sought to unite all people of the German culture, language or "race" within one great empire. The Führer pushed this idea to the maximum by stating that once these people were united, he would extend the territory to acquire the land necessary for the survival of his people.
- The League of Nations, created in 1919 at the signing of the Treaty of Versailles in order to prevent further global conflict, failed to restore the situation as it had no leverage.
- The Rome-Berlin-Tokyo Axis, an economic and military alliance between Italy, Nazi Germany and the Japanese Empire, was created in September 1940.
- The rearmament of the German troops would commence once Adolf Hitler had come to power, while the production of armament factories was kept to a minimum following the agreements of the Treaty of Versailles. The Führer hoped to revive the economy of the country that was previously overcome, firstly by debts owed to the victorious nations of the First World War, and secondly by the 1929 crisis.

All of these factors made a war on the European continent

inevitable. Although France and the United Kingdom remained relatively inactive during the annexation of Austria (March 1938) and Czechoslovakia (March 1939) by Germany, they issued the country with an ultimatum on 1 September 1939, when the armies of Adolf Hitler invaded part of Poland, marking the beginning of the Second World War.

THE STAKES IN THE BATTLE OF THE ATLANTIC

The Battle of the Atlantic began on 3 September 1939. As soon as he heard of the ultimatums issued against him, Adolf Hitler ordered the establishment of measures to paralyze all UK imports transiting the Atlantic. On the eve of the conflict, Britain was indeed at the head of a major colonial empire, whose economy and industry were largely based on the delivery of raw materials from its colonies. Therefore, the Germans wanted to prevent any supplies brought by sea in order to paralyze the economy, starving its people, and to force the government to surrender.

GOOD TO KNOW

The Atlantic had also been the scene of fighting during the First World War. Since the outbreak of the conflict, Britain had imposed a naval blockade of Germany to undermine the country's war economy. Therefore, fearing a direct confrontation with the Royal Navy, very powerful at the time, the German staff chose to confine its High Seas Fleet to its bases in the Baltic Sea. In 1916, an exit attempt resulted in the greatest naval battle of the First World War, which involved more than 200 ships: the Battle of Jutland (31 May-1 June). Despite a German tactical victory – the British losses were indeed much larger – it was Britain who emerged victorious as the German fleet was forced to turn around and did not try any new attempts before the end of the war.

However, the Germans had not said their final words and tried in turn to impose a blockade on the UK using a new machine: submarines. Although the first operation was launched in 1915, it was not until February 1917 that unrestricted submarine warfare appeared, constituting a nightmare for the Britons who lost many men and ships.

THE GERMANY NAVY IN THE DAWN OF WORLD WAR II

However, a major problem prevented the Germans from implementing their plan for controlling the Atlantic Ocean and setting up a blockade of the United Kingdom. Indeed, following the Treaty of Versailles, there were restrictions on the German forces' armaments. The powerful army of 1918 was transformed into a defense army in order to minimize its ability to trigger a new conflict. But when Hitler came to power in 1933, he dreamed of giving Germany a vast empire. In order for this to come true, he needed a significant fighting force, which he currently lacked. The German Navy had only a few small warships, most of which were too old, with a maximum tonnage (i.e. the sum of the weights of all the ships in the fleet) that could not exceed 10 000 tons. The maximum tonnage authorized for the entire German fleet was limited to 108 000 tons, which, given the military standards of the time, was almost insignificant and did not leave the Führer with many possibilities. However, after several negotiations, Adolf Hitler managed to reach an agreement with the British government, allowing him to set up a fleet of up to 35% of the tonnage of the surface fleet and 45% of the tonnage of the anti-surface fleet of the Royal Navy.

Therefore, during the thirties, the German construction sites were put back in service to produce new warships. From an economic point of view, the German chancellor used shipyards to create jobs in Germany, whose economy was moribund. Despite his efforts, on the eve of the conflict, the tonnage of the British fleet remained eight times larger than that of the German fleet.

THE BRITISH NAVY: A GIANT WITH FEET OF CLAY?

Building a fleet to rival that of the British was almost impossible. In fact, Britain was the head of the first colonial power in the world, which required a navy capable of protecting its colonies and the maritime routes leading to it. It was Britain who had the greatest naval force on the eve of World War II. However, this force was not without its flaws:

- It was aging and no longer adapted to the new naval battles that would emerge during the Second World War;
- It did not have enough escort vessels, the role of which was to protect other ships from attacks by submarines;

- Due to the extent of the British colonial empire, it was spread around the globe to ensure the protection of its possessions.

COMMANDERS AND LEADERS

ERICH RAEDER, GERMAN ADMIRAL

Erich Raeder was born in 1876 in the suburbs of Hamburg (northern Germany). As soon as he had completed his secondary education, he began a career in the German Navy. During the First World War, he was part of the staff of Admiral Franz von Hipper (1863-1932), with whom he participated in several battles against the Royal Navy. In 1925, he obtained the rank of vice admiral, then became admiral three years later.

Erich Raeder and Adolf Hitler, photo taken in 1934.

When Adolf Hitler came to power, he included Erich Raeder in his plan for the restoration of the German fleet, Plan Z, which involved building six battleships, two aircraft carriers, 225 submarines and numerous cruisers and destroyers. Hitler also asked him for his advice when defining the guidelines to be followed by the *Kriegsmarine* (German Navy) in the event of major naval warfare. Erich Raeder advised him to favor the construction of large surface warships over submarines. In 1936, he was appointed commander-in-chief of the German Navy and received the prestigious title of Grand Admiral three years later.

He then advised the Führer to invade Norway and Denmark in 1940, to prevent the British and the French from installing bases there and to secure the trade route of the Swedish iron ore, essential to the German war industry. But, little by little, Erich Raeder lost his influence on Adolf Hitler, because his surface ships proved less effective than he had predicted before the war. Indeed, several setbacks, such as the loss of the *Bismarck*, the pride and joy of the German navy, and the defeat at the Battle of Barents (31 December 1942), led to him losing his credibility due to the successes of the submarines. He resigned on 30 January 1943 and was replaced by Karl Dönitz. Following his departure and his loss of influence with the Führer, Erich Raeder spent the rest of the war without any real function and saw that he was being distanced from power. After the conflict, the Nuremberg Trials in 1946 condemned him to life imprisonment for his participation in the rearmament of Germany, which was forbidden by the Treaty of Versailles. However, Erich Raeder was released in September 1955 due to his deteriorating health and he died five years later.

KARL DÖNITZ, GERMAN ADMIRAL

Picture of (from left to right) Franz Xaver Dorsch (German civil engineer,1899-1986), Albert Speer (German statesman and architect, 1905-1981) and Karl Dönitz.

Karl Dönitz, officer of the German Navy, was born in 1891 in Berlin. He joined the Navy in 1910. During the First World War, he served on a cruiser in the Mediterranean and the Black Sea, before receiving submariner training in 1916. From 1917, he fought from a submarine and was then awarded command of the *UC-25* between March and September 1918. In October, he was captured by the British after his appointment as commander of the *UB-68*. Released after the war, he returned to Germany in 1920 and supported the ideas of the Nazi party.

Highly regarded by Adolf Hitler – who would designate him as his successor at the head of the Third Reich before committing suicide in 1945 –, he tried to convince the Führer to convert the *Kriegsmarine* into a huge underwater battle fleet and abandon the big surface ships built by Erich Raeder. In 1936, he became head of the German submarine fleet. Seeing the efficiency of the *U-Boot* (abbreviation of *Unterseeboot*, meaning "submarine") of Karl Dönitz in the Battle of the Atlantic, Adolf Hitler appointed him head of the *Kriegsmarine* after the resignation of Erich Raeder.

Therefore, he sought to develop the tactic known as the *Rudeltaktik* ("tactical packs") which consisted of a group attack of the German submarines on the Allied convoys. This strategy would, for a time, tip the balance in favor of the German side in the Battle of the Atlantic.

GOOD TO KNOW

In 1936, Germany signed the London Convention,

which prohibited extensive submarine warfare due to the devastation caused during the First World War. Although Adolf Hitler and Erich Raeder were initially inclined to respect this principle, which partly explains why the spotlight was given to the production of surface ships, stinging setbacks to the *Kriegsmarine* in the early years of the conflict and the success won by the U-Boats pushed the Führer to further develop underwater weapons.

Until the end of the war, Karl Dönitz held the position of head of the Germany Navy. On the death of Adolf Hitler, he became head of what remained of the Third Reich and decided to start negotiating peace with the Western Allies. It was on his orders that General Alfred Jodl (1890-1946) would sign the surrender of Germany in Reims on 7 May 1945.

Karl Dönitz was then arrested and tried at Nuremberg. He was sentenced to ten years in prison, after which he led a quiet life before dying of a heart attack in 1980.

SIR MAX KENNEDY HORTON, BRITISH ADMIRAL

Sir Max Kennedy Horton.

Born in Rhosneigr (North Wales) in 1883, Sir Max Kennedy Horton was a senior officer in the British Navy. He entered the Royal Navy in 1898, rising gradually through the ranks of the hierarchy and, from September 1914, commanded a submarine. He participated in many operations during the

First World War in the North Sea and the Baltic Sea.

In 1932, he was appointed Rear-Admiral, then Vice Admiral and became head of the reserve fleet five years later. When World War II broke out, he participated in the defense of Britain, before becoming head of the submarine fleet in January 1940. On 17 November 1942, he was appointed Western Approaches Command and was in charge of ships in the Atlantic area, becoming the primary commander of the Royal Navy during the Battle of the Atlantic.

He quickly introduced new tactics to decrease the number of Allied ships sunk by the German forces, especially by the U-Boats of Karl Dönitz. According to him, as it was impossible to avoid the German submarine groups, it was therefore necessary to fight them. To do this, Max Kennedy Horton intensified the training of crews on the escort vessels of the Allied convoys. He also created rapid support units that could come to reinforce the escorts if a submarine attack became imminent. This new approach would limit the number of ships sunk by submarines in the Atlantic.

At the end of the war, Max Kennedy Horton requested his retirement. Therefore, he left the Royal Navy and was ordained as Knight Grand Cross of the Order of the Bath, an honor granted to British soldiers and civil servants. He died peacefully in 1951.

ERNEST KING, AMERICAN ADMIRAL

Ernest King.

Born in 1878, Ernest King was an American Admiral commanding the forces of the U.S. Navy during the Battle of the Atlantic. In 1897, he enrolled at the Naval Academy in Annapolis and took part in the conflicts in which the United States participated of the Spanish-American War (April-August 1898) and the Mexican Revolution (American intervention in Veracruz in 1914), allowing him to gain some experience.

During the First World War, he served with Vice Admiral Henry Mayo (1856-1937) and participated in several operations of the Royal Navy as an observer. After the war, Ernest King was transferred to the American submarine fleet with the rank of captain, a position he held from 1923 to 1925. He was then posted in naval aviation, an air component of the U.S. Navy. From there, he rose through the ranks to become commander of the Naval Air Force in 1936 and Vice Admiral two years later. Upon the entry of the United States into the war in 1941, he was appointed commander of the American fleet. In 1942, he was appointed Chief of Naval Operations and participated in the Battle of the Atlantic. It was also he who organized the American convoys and the routing of the U.S. troops and equipment in Europe.

Admiral Ernest King left the Navy at the end of 1945, but was recalled to be an advisor on behalf of the Secretariat for the U.S. Navy. He died of a heart attack in 1956.

ANALYSIS OF THE BATTLE

THE START OF THE BATTLE

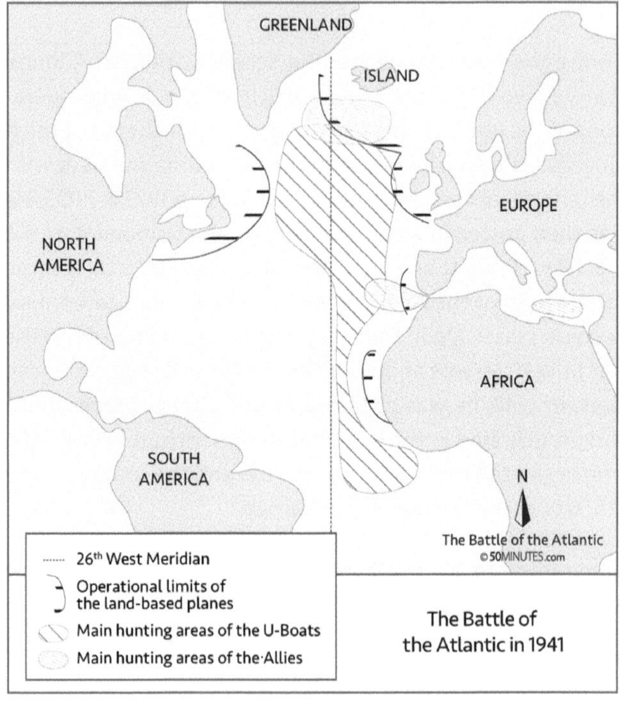

The Battle of
the Atlantic in 1941

The Battle of the Atlantic began on the first day of the announcement of the state of war between Britain, France and Nazi Germany. The first victims were the passengers on the liner *Athenia*, torpedoed by the *U-30* U-Boat. Two days later, the SS Royal Spectrum, a British freighter in the dark waters of the Atlantic, fell victim to the *U-48*. These first two losses were very representative of what the Battle of the Atlantic would become: a fierce struggle between the Allied ships crossing the Atlantic and the submarines of the Third Reich.

On the first day of the war, the German fleet was mainly composed of 57 submarines and a few cruisers, along with ships inherited from the First World War. Karl Dönitz, who realized how the fight against the Allies would develop, said that it would take about 300 submarines to carry out the mission and force Britain to surrender. The small number of U-Boats available at the beginning of the conflict showed the first tactical error of the German Admiralty. Adolf Hitler, wanting to satisfy his two naval advisers, Erich Raeder and Karl Dönitz, had not clearly determined the question of the direction to be taken by the *Kreigsmarine*. Consequently, Germany did not have a sufficient number of submarines to satisfy its ambitions and its surface fleet was not large enough to cause concern for the Allied navies. Several vessels still won successes, such as the *Graf Spee* cruiser which destroyed nine ships before being sabotaged in December 1939, or even the seemingly harmless merchant ships which concealed weapons to engage in other commercial ships.

Before the start of the war, Adolf Hitler knew that, in order to be able to maneuver in the Atlantic where the Allied ships were abundant, submarines, which came from the Baltic Sea, must pass northern Scotland. However, the models available to him did not have enough autonomy to make such a journey. It was therefore vital to seize the French ports to gain direct access to the Atlantic Ocean and thus keep out the Allied ships. The capture of France from June 1940 therefore gave the Germans the coastal territories as it desired. Thus, Karl Dönitz obtained the means to deploy his submarines and attack the transatlantic convoys more easily. Submarine bases were then created on the French Atlantic coast (Brest, Lorient, La Rochelle, Saint-Nazaire and Bordeaux). Although the German fleet was confined to its home in the early months of the conflict, this capture gave it the edge in the Battle of the Atlantic: until 1941-1942, the German forces gained multiple successes and the Allied losses were numerous.

GOOD TO KNOW

In order to relieve the British Navy, the United States established a neutral zone in April 1941 covering the whole of the Atlantic Ocean west of the 26th West Meridian (meridian passing west of Iceland and east of Brazil), an area in which its fleet protected the convoys headed to Britain. At a time when the United States had not yet entered the war, this decision had the advantage of dissuading the German submarines from attacking in the area and allowing the British to redeploy their escorts in other parts of the Atlantic. When they entered the war in December 1941, the neutral zone became an open hunting ground for German submarines, which won several successes, as the Allied navies first revealed themselves unable to defend such a large area.

THE WOLF PACK TACTIC

Despite the small numbers of the German forces, the British Navy was far behind in terms of technology and did not have, from the outbreak of the conflict, ships that were suitable for escorting their convoys and fighting against underwater attacks. This situation greatly facilitated the work of the U-Boats, allowing them to wreak havoc in the first months of the war.

The Allied situation was made all the more critical when Admiral Karl Dönitz developed, in October 1940, what he called "wolf pack" tactics, which consisted of grouping submarines into "packs" composed of between three and thirty submarines, separated by a few nautical miles (one nautical mile equals approximately 1 850 meters). When one of the U-Boats saw an Allied convoy, it gave the grouping signal to the other members of its pack. The submarine then followed the trail of radio waves emitted by the one who spotted the potential target. Once the group had reformed, the "wolves" attacked the convoy, usually at night and on the surface. However, although these attacks were grouped, they were not coordinated.

It was only in a war directive dated 6 February 1941 that Adolf Hitler recognized, firstly that submarine warfare was the best way of undermining the British economy and crippling the war efforts of the Allies, and secondly that it was essential to attack the merchant ships. He therefore substantially increased the number of U-Boats in operation in the Atlantic. However, the Führer committed a strategic error by assigning the *Luftwaffe*, the German air force under the command of Hermann Goering (German Marshal and politician, 1893-1946), the task of bombing the British cities, instead of ordering it to make planes available for the *Kriegsmarine* to attack and identify Allied convoys in the Atlantic. The invasion of Russia in June 1941 did not help the situation, since much of the *Luftwaffe* was dispatched to the Eastern Front, thus depriving the Germans of a major asset in the Battle of the Atlantic.

THE "BLACK HOLE" AND THE LIVING CONDITIONS OF SEAFARERS AT THE HEART OF THE BATTLE

An area of the Atlantic Ocean, known as the "Black Hole", was reported to be the favorite hunting ground of the "wolves" of Karl Dönitz. This was a wide ocean area where Allied ships could not count on any help from aviation, because the British and Canadians did not have, at that time, planes with a sufficient range to cover and survey that part of the ocean. Allied convoys were then left to their own devices and could not be warned of the presence of German submarines. The danger was omnipresent and the lives of the men onboard were very difficult. The stress, the constant tension and the fatigue that resulted from it were added to the bad weather, the cold and the constantly rough seas.

The fate of the German submariners was no more enviable. Indeed, they were subjected to containment and lack of space. The rare surfacing of the U-Boats was usually at night and was intended to replenish oxygen levels. In addition, during the fighting, the German sailors knew that any entry of water into their submarine was likely to be fatal. This was partly due to the fact that electric batteries allowing the U-Boats to sail underwater contained acid, which, when in contact with water, emitted deadly gases.

THE FIRST DIFFICULTIES FOR THE *KRIEGSMARINE*

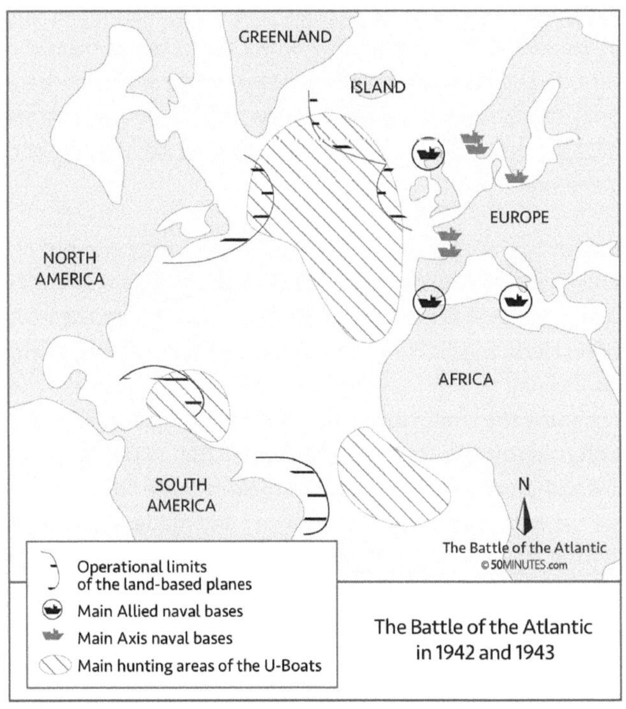

The Battle of the Atlantic in 1942 and 1943

While the U-Boats won some victories in the Atlantic Ocean, several events tarnished the enthusiasm in the German camp. In May 1941, the *U-110* was forced to return to the surface and was captured by Allied escorts. They were then able to discover the codes of the German encryption machine, the famous Enigma machine, and all accompanying documents (meteorological codes, abbreviations, etc.). This discovery allowed the Allies to decode some of the messages that the German ships sent to their Admiralty, and thus to know the locations of the submarines of the *Kriegsmarine*. They could now divert the convoys from the German patrols and hunt them down. However, in February 1942, the Germans adopted a new model of the Enigma machine, which would be discovered by the Allies at the end of the year.

Moreover, the organization of the German army was not arranged to help the *Kriegsmarine*. Indeed, it had no aircrafts to protect its ships, identify Allied convoys or try to destroy them. Hermann Goering, commander of the *Luftwaffe*, was not inclined to provide equipment to the Navy as he did not recognize the importance of its task during the war and preferred to promote the bombings of cities in the center of England. However, this was a strategic mistake because, unlike the Nazi forces, the British Army had made an airborne division available to the Royal Navy that depended directly on the Admiralty, able to spot the U-Boats and attack them. The role of the British aircrafts would become increasingly important during the battle.

The German Admiralty also faced the relative ineffectiveness of the *Regia Marina*, which was at their disposal since Benito Mussolini gave them access to his own fleet of submarines. But these vessels, designed to sail in the Mediterranean, were ill-suited for navigation and combat in water as capricious as the Atlantic Ocean. Thus, the Italians could play only a minor role in the Atlantic campaign.

On 27 May, the German population experienced a new disappointment when it learned of the destruction of the *Bismarck*, a brand-new battleship that was the pride of the nation. This event demonstrated to Germany that Eric Raeder was wrong and that victory would not come from surface vessels.

The final element that changed the game of the fighting in the Atlantic in 1941 was the entry of the United Stated into the war in December, which joined with the British and the Canadians to monitor the waterways of the Atlantic.

THE "WOLVES" TAKE THE BULL BY THE HORNS

Although the Americans stated that they wanted to retain the trade routes of the Atlantic, they were slow to organize escorts for their convoys, leaving the U-Boats and even Italian submarines to be sent along the American coast as they continued their operations. No less than 200 merchant ships were sunk by the submarines of the Axis in the first months of 1942, without encountering serious resistance from the U.S. forces.

This is partly explained by the fact that the Allies were taken by surprise by the Germans who, having discovered that the British were able to decipher their messages, had changed the Enigma machine and introduced new codes. It was not until December 1942 that the Allies could once again decrypt the messages sent by the German forces in the Atlantic.

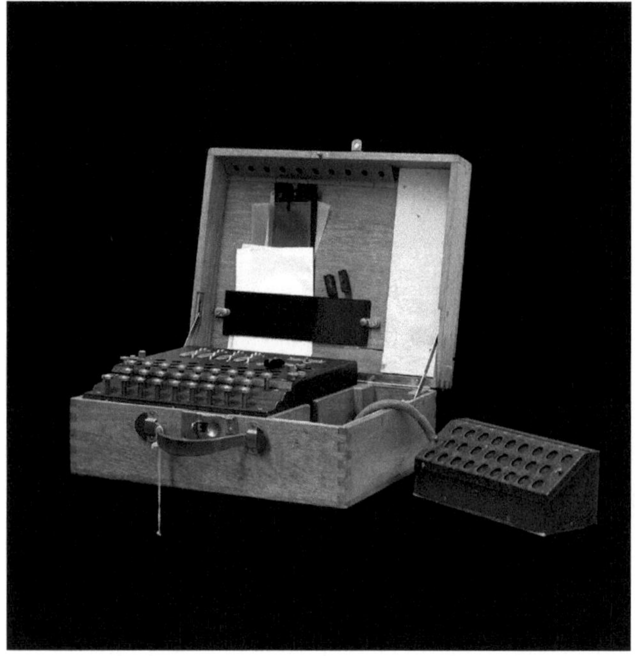

Cryptanalysis of the Enigma machine enabled the Allies to decipher substantial amounts of secret German messages

Thanks to the success of the submarines, Karl Dönitz saw his U-Boat forces increase significantly. In June 1942, he had over 300 submarines, plus a further 100 in December. However, they were not used simultaneously. Indeed, some of them were particularly devoted to the training of crews in the Baltic Sea. In addition, this increase in manpower went hand in hand with the launch of new machines. Thus, from the winter of 1941-1942, special submarines designed to supply diesel and ammunition to the U-Boats appeared on the high seas, allowing them to remain active longer.

THE END OF GERMAN HOPES

However, the situation for the commander of the German submarine forces and his crew was far from ideal because the Allies made every effort to reduce their losses and fight effectively against the German submarines: the convoys were protected; the escorts were better prepared by Max Kennedy Horton and Ernest Joseph King; air cover was greater; new submarine grenades were used; radars and sonars had been improved, etc. Thus, although 1942 marked the peak of the domination of the German submarines in the Atlantic, the situation was now about to change. While the U.S. industry produced standardized vessels to replace the losses incurred, the Germans were finding it increasingly difficult to keep up.

Faced with the growing number of casualties among his men and a diminution of their effectiveness, Karl Dönitz, then commander of the *Kriegsmarine*, removed most of his U-Boats from the Atlantic in the summer of 1943, while waiting for new, more sophisticated models. However, these new weapons would never appear, or at least not until it was too late, and the German fleet would no longer be able to cause concern for the Allied fleets.

THE OUTCOME OF THE BATTLE

Finally, although the Battle of the Atlantic continued until May 1945, the outcome was certain once the bulk of the German submarine fleet was withdrawn from the Atlantic.

Four key factors helped the Allies to achieve victory in this terrible sea battle:

- The entry into the war of the United States, which, along with putting new warships at the service of the Allies, especially allowed for the production of significant amounts of material. Their powerful standardized industry aimed to produce more ships than the Germans could sink.
- The massive use of aviation to hunt down the German submarines that surfaced.
- Scientific advances that allowed the Allies, from 1942 to 1943, to obtain an advantage through more efficient equipment. The Allied fleets, which were originally unprepared for a war against submarines, developed during the battle a whole arsenal of measures enabling them to send as many U-Boats to the bottom of the sea as they did to the Allied ships.
- Finally, the deciphering of some German communications allowed them to identify numerous submarines.

As for the outcome of this battle, its price was heavy, both in terms of men and material. The Allies suffered the loss of approximately 45 000 men, over 2 500 merchant ships and 175 warships. Meanwhile, the Germans lost most of their large surface ships and all their crews, representing thousands of sailors. The few ships that had not been destroyed in the ports would be immobilized and captured during the Liberation. However, it was the submariners that paid the highest price: of approximately 40 000 men, 25 000 were killed and 5 000 were captured by the Allies. With regards to materials, of the 830 submarines involved, about 700 were destroyed.

Painting of the Battle of the Atlantic.

REPERCUSSIONS OF THE BATTLE

THE CONSEQUENCES IN THE AFTERMATH OF THE CONFLICT

Although the German attacks on the Allied ships in the Atlantic continued until the end of the war, the Germans were no longer able to stop or even slow the extraordinary number of men and the routing of equipment from the American continent to the United Kingdom and Africa. Thus, a direct consequence of the withdrawal of German forces from the Atlantic in 1943 was the opportunity for the Allies to prepare the Normandy invasion and thus open a new front to begin the liberation of occupied Europe. This operation would lead to the landings of 6 June 1944, which required months of preparation and the displacement of a huge number of troops and equipment from the United States and Canada. All of this would have been impossible, without the suffering of incalculable human and material losses, if the Germans had been able to maintain their fleet of U-Boats at full strength in the Atlantic Ocean.

In addition, in the Pacific, the Americans quickly used the ideas and tactics of Karl Dönitz for their own benefit, in order to undermine the Japanese power. Thus, there would be "wolf packs" of the U.S. submarines in the Pacific which aimed to sink as many Japanese ships as possible to block the Japanese economy.

This conflict also allowed Canada, which at the dawn of World War II had a paltry navy, to acquire new naval vessels.

In the same vein, the British Army was forced to renovate and bring the Royal Navy up to date, which possessed vessels that could have been considered as aging.

Finally, the Battle of the Atlantic would also allow some American ports to expand when the demand for merchant ships was most significant. Shipbuilding and construction sites appeared particularly on the East Coast of the United States.

TOWARDS A NEW NAVAL WARFARE

It is clear that the battle profoundly changed the way of thinking about Navy war. Ever since, many war fleets equipped themselves with submarines to which the staffs granted more and more importance. In the final years of the war, the Germans also brought many improvements to their U-Boats, but they were too late and did not allow Karl Dönitz to regain the advantage in a battle which he lost by removing most of his submarine fleet from the Atlantic in the summer of 1943. Among the innovations, the Germans developed a submarine that could stay submerged longer and could navigate more quickly underwater. At the end of the war, these new technologies were recovered by the victorious states.

On the Allied side, many innovations also emerged. Thus, the Allies – and the Germans to some extent – contributed to the creation and development of the radar system. Early in the war, they were still far from perfect and did not produce the expected results. For example, at the beginning of the conflict, they could not identify the U-Boats that surfaced.

Similarly, anti-submarine grenades underwent profound changes during the Battle of the Atlantic. Before this clash, a ship could only launch grenades from the rear, more rarely from the flanks, but for a very short distance. The ship was therefore forced to perform many maneuvers to position themselves in relation to the target submarine – maneuvers which could also put the vessel in danger. The emergence of systems such as the "hedgehog" or the "squid" revolutionized anti-submarine warfare by allowing warships to launch charges and explosives 30 meters away with the "hedgehog" and 100 meters with the "squid" systems, which also posed many problems for the German submariners in the last years of the Battle of the Atlantic.

The final remarkable innovation to appear during the clash was the torpedo homing, which is owed to the Americans. These models were guided acoustically, based on the noise emitted by the propeller of a submarine or a surface vessel. Shortly after, the Germans also created their own torpedo homing model, also based on the noise produced by the propellers.

ECOLOGICAL CONSEQUENCES

Unfortunately, this battle had consequences on the oceans which are still visible today. The seabed was indeed polluted by shipwrecks and more particularly due to the many German submarines that sank in the Atlantic waters during the clashes. These vessels, which contained many toxic substances (mercury, acid, heavy metals, etc.), have been

scattered in the ocean for decades and are gradually relea-
sing these substances. This phenomenon may result in the
contamination of the aquatic environment located around
the wrecks and therefore represents a risk to the Atlantic
ecosystem. Some solutions are being considered, including
the construction of domes or boxes to be placed around the
debris to stem the leakage of harmful substances.

SUMMARY

- The Battle of the Atlantic, with 68 months of uninterrupted battle between the European and American continents, was the longest battle of the Second World War. It was revealed to be extremely challenging, both in human and financial terms, with tens of thousands of victims in each camp, and millions of tons of materials sent to the bottom of the ocean.
- The duration of the battle was so impressive because the stakes were essential for the future outcome of the

conflict. Indeed, in order to bend the Allies, Hitler knew that he must cut off all lines of communication and assistance transport from the American continent to the British Isles. Thus, the German Navy would constantly try to sink as many vessels as possible on the waterways of the Atlantic Ocean.

- However, the failure of the German blockade would enable the Allies to deliver enough men and equipment to open a new land front in occupied Europe and, ultimately, to deliver the final blow to Nazi Germany.
- The rearmament – a violation of the terms of the Treaty of Versailles -, modernization and new tactics, namely the underwater tactics of the *Kriegsmarine*, helped by the lack of effectiveness of the Allied convoy escorts, allowed the Axis forces to undermine the Allies for a time and tip the balance in their favor.
- However, the discovery of the encryption codes of the German submarine communication, the redistribution of the escorts allocated to their convoys, the control of the airspace over the Atlantic and the tenacity of their men finally gave the advantage to the Allied forces. Therefore, Germany could no longer manage to contain the flow of materials transported from the United States and Canada.
- The Battle of the Atlantic was witness to scientific and technological advances in many fields. It also changed the military vision of naval combat and therefore revolutionized it.
- However, although the battle led to technological advances, it nevertheless caused serious ecological problems that are still unresolved, due to the many ships

that were sent to the bottom of the sea during this titanic conflict.

We want to hear from you!
Leave a comment on your online library
and share your favourite books on social media!

FIND OUT MORE

BIBLIOGRAPHY

- Bishop, C. (2012) *Kriegsmarine U-Boats*. London: Amber Books.
- Campbell, J. (1985) *Naval Weapons of World War II*. Annapolis: Naval Institute Press.
- Cartier R. (1965) *La Seconde Guerre mondiale*. Paris: Larousse Paris-Match.
- Malbosc, G. (2011) *La bataille de l'Atlantique (1939-1945). La victoire logistique et celle du renseignement, clés de la victoire des armes*. Paris: Economica.
- Peillard, L. (1974) *La bataille de l'Atlantique*. Paris: Robert Laffont.
- Roper-Trevor, H. (2004) *Hitler's War Directives 1939-1945*. Edinburgh: Birlinn Limited.
- Vallaud, P. (2004) *La Seconde Guerre mondiale*. Paris: Acropole.
- Uboat.net (No date) *About uboat.net*. [Online]. [Accessed 7 December 2016]. Available from: <http://www.uboat.net/>

ADDITIONAL SOURCES

- Brown, D. (2007) *Atlantic Escorts, Ships, Weapons & Tactics in World War II*. Barnsley: Seaforth Publishing.
- Dimbleby, J. (2016) *The Battle of the Atlantic: How the Allies Won the War*. London: Penguin.
- Hague, A. (2000) *The Allied Convoy System*. Ontario: Vanwell Publishing.

- Milner, M. (2011) *Battle of the Atlantic*. Abingdon: History Press.
- Nesbit, R.C. (2008) *Ultra versus U-Boats. Enigma Decrypts in the National Archives*. Barnsley: Pen and Sword Military.
- Syrett, D. (1994) *The Defeat of the German U-Boats. The Battle of the Atlantic*. Columbia, University of South Carolina Press.

ICONOGRAPHIC SOURCES

- Erich Raeder and Adolf Hitler, photo taken in 1934. © German Federal Archives.
- Photo of Franz Xaver Dorsch, Albert Speer and Karl Dönitz. Royalty-free reproduction picture. © German Federal Archives.
- Sir Max Kennedy Horton. Royalty free reproduction picture. © Royal Navy official photographer.
- Ernest King. Royalty-free reproduction picture.
- Enigma machine. Royalty-free reproduction picture
- Painting of the Battle of the Atlantic. Royalty-free reproduction picture.

DOCUMENTARIES

- *Doenitz vs. Horton*. (2002) [Documentary]. Jonathan Martin. Dir. USA.
- *La Bataille de l'Atlantique*. (2004) [Documentary]. René-Jean Bouyer. Dir. France.
- *Les Grandes Batailles : la bataille de l'Atlantique*. (2010) [Documentary]. Daniel Costelle. Dir. France.

MUSEUMS AND COMMEMORATIVE BUILDINGS

- The Laboe Naval Memorial, a monument dedicated to the German marine victims of the First World War and all the missing sailors of the Second World War (Germany).
- The Western Approaches Museum, located in the former headquarters of the Western Approaches, Liverpool (England).
- The Maritime Museum of the Atlantic, Halifax (Canada).